AF437409

PAOLO DI TUCCIPHOTO

My heartfelt thanks to Antonio Ciano and Carlo Di Nitto, custodians of precious memories, for sharing news and recollections with me, and to my friend Sabina Mitrano, for the encouragement and for helping me retrieve a seemingly untraceable text.

On the cover: Santo Spirito Monastery of Zannone in Gaeta, photo by Donatella de' Spagnolis
Photos by: Lino Sorabella p. 16; Paolo Di Tucci p. 20-27, 30-34, 44-54, 56-60, 68-70, 74-77, 80-88, 101-105; Jason R. Forbus p. 19, 28-29, 55, 63, 66-67, 71-72, 78, 89-99, 106, 116-117; Donatella de' Spagnolis pp. 38-43; Francesco Sinopoli pp. 64-65.
Photo captions, where not specified otherwise, by Lino sorabella
Editor-in-Chief: Jason R. Forbus
Graphic design and layout: Sara Calmosi

Original Italian edition published by Ali Ribelli Edizioni, 2019 © English edition 2023 ©
Ventus Press
Ali Ribelli Edizioni Group
www.aliribelli.com – redazione@aliribelli.com

Ventus Press, operating under the Ali Ribelli Edizioni group (Rebel Wings Publishing), is distributed worldwide through IngramSpark.

JASON R. FORBUS

HIDDEN TREASURES IN GAETA

Preface by Gennaro Tallini

| Author's Note

This book is an act of love towards the hidden and forgotten Gaeta.

Those fortunate enough to live in or visit the city are enchanted by its sea, its churches and monuments, its breathtaking landscapes...

However, looking beyond the postcard – or Instagram reel – one discovers a concealed city: remnants of Roman structures, monasteries and medieval churches, sites of historical and cultural interest unknown to mass tourism, abandoned in the silence of the outskirts and the countryside.

Following the release of the original Italian edition of this book, surveyor Marco Sasso and I meticulously compiled a comprehensive list pinpointing the precise cadastral parcels where the archaeological sites mentioned in this book can be found. This list was duly submitted to the municipality of Gaeta and the designated officials at the Art Superintendency of the Latina and Frosinone Provinces. However, after two years, there has been no discernible progress, and it seems that this country is preoccupied with preserving the more prominent sites, while the "out of sight, out of mind" ruins are overlooked.

Hidden Treasures in Gaeta has a primary goal of acquainting the people of Gaeta, both the younger and older generations, with their rich heritage, aiming to ignite their curiosity and foster love for their native land. Yet, it also serves as a poignant cry for help emanating from archaeological sites facing imminent obliteration unless swift action is taken.

Additionally, this book serves as an opportunity to engage with tourists, inspiring them to explore these ancient and contemporary sites in Gaeta. We encourage visitors to do so with the proper caution and in the company of expert, licensed guides. These sites not only encapsulate the history of Gaeta, but also offer a glimpse into its present and, possibly, its future.

My hope is that the historical insights woven alongside the photographs of the visited sites, the narrative, and the poetry will transform this book into a distinctive postcard, setting it apart from the typical ones on display. The book is designed to offer an experience that transcends mere viewing; it invites readers to deeply feel the profound significance and soul-healing power of the hidden beauty that surrounds us.

Jason R. Forbus

To Drake Edward and David Finn Forbus:
Be explorers of life

| Table of Contents

"Who were your forebears?" With this reference to Dante's famous verse (*Inferno*, Canto XI), I aim to introduce Jason Forbus' remarkable book. I am deeply grateful to him for inviting me to write its preface, even though I may not be the most fitting choice, especially as I'm not a "local historian."

So why did I find this concise collection of thoughts and targeted reflections, a written record of images that only the human mind, in all its complexity and precision, can depict in all their beauty and desolation, so captivating? There are numerous answers, and beyond answers, there linger questions – questions that are more numerous and challenging to resolve than the issues of preservation, knowledge, and study that these antiquities pose for discussion, for posterity, and for scholars and enthusiasts alike. Nonetheless, despite the limited space at my disposal, I will endeavor to address these matters and offer, I hope, comprehensive and illuminating responses to what this text can offer, both to the less experienced reader, and to the most discerning and cultured.

As a philologist, especially concerned with antiquities, the interplay between antiquities and classical and modern traditions, and antiquarian writings of the Renaissance era, it is my professional duty to remind the reader (regardless of their level of knowledge and expertise) that the imperative to transmit knowledge about places, a practice as old as humanity itself, is a matter of historical consciousness and a testament to belonging. Understanding the history of the places where one acts and lives daily is so deeply intertwined with human life that neglecting this connection is akin to committing social suicide. Conversely, erasing the memory of a historical dimension (not just historical events themselves) or failing to comprehend the reasons behind a phenomenon is a form of cultural suicide.

Unfortunately, in today's world (and Gaeta's history offers daily examples and proof of this), not only is the understanding and remembrance neglected (meaning, understanding the past and remembering it as it once was when it was present), but there is also a reluctance to study and preserve what has been passed down and bequeathed as a testament to a unique civilization and cultural expression. Neglect is, regrettably, not just a result of ignorance; it is also a glaring indication of the disconnect that currently exists between what is observed and its necessary economic utility. Not only are ruins reduced to mere fragments of structures, but even the mundane aspects of daily life are subjected to various forms of abandonment and neglect. The continuous evasion of regulations then distorts the concept of restoration into an erroneous interpretation that attempts to view the artifact as it existed in antiquity while adapting it to the functionalities of the contemporary world. This often results in a monstrosity that has lost its original meaning and, essentially, relegates the ancient to the status of a useless object, at best visible behind a display case.

Nowadays, unfortunately (and Gaeta's history doesn't shy away from providing us with daily examples of this), not only is there a reluctance to understand and remember (meaning, comprehending the past and remembering it as it was when it was present), but there is also a reluctance to study and preserve what has been passed down and delivered as a testament to a unique civilization and cultural expression. Neglect is, regrettably, not just a result of ignorance; it is also a glaring indication of the disconnect that currently exists between what is observed and its necessary economic utility. Not only are ruins reduced to mere fragments of structures, but even the mundane aspects of daily life are subjected to various forms of abandonment and neglect. The continuous evasion of regulations then distorts the concept of restoration into an erroneous interpretation that attempts to view the artifact as it existed in antiquity while adapting it to the functionalities of the contemporary world. This often results in a monstrosity that has lost its original meaning and, essentially, relegates the ancient to the status of a useless object, at best visible behind a display case.

It may be argued that these are clichés, but this is the only approach that allows us (playing on words) to "cross the street" and reconstruct the mosaic that is the history of a family, a street, a monument, a neighborhood, or an entire city.

I mentioned earlier that reading this book left me with more questions than answers. These questions are not of an architectural, archaeological, or simply historical nature, but rather pertain to the role of these three forms of human knowledge in relation to memory throughout the ages. Merely having the sea, enjoying a "tiella" (as a well-known internet title proclaims), sailing on a boat, or partaking in "fare le bottiglie," all actions deeply ingrained in the average Gaetan's familial tradition and experienced exhaustively during their own childhood, is insufficient. These actions remain superficial and self-contained unless one recognizes in them their commemorative significance and the historical necessity of passing down to future generations the essence of a civilization that was partly agrarian and piscatorial and that, over the centuries, managed to preserve its own language (not merely a dialect), maintain a consciousness of its origins and millennia-long history, jealously safeguard precious artifacts, and produce literary masterpieces and works of humanistic and Renaissance art. It's only in recent decades that this connection with the past has been willfully severed, turning away and reducing it to mere "stones inside and out", a self-absolving axiom that placates consciences after each abuse.

So, who are our ancestors, then? Who were those who walked this land, were born, lived, worked, fought, and died within the borders of this city, whose history predates even that of Rome? Do its inhabitants recognize this *genos*, this lineage, and their connection to a millennia-old history? These are the initial questions that linger in my mind after reading, emerging immediately as the first images of arches, frescoes weathered by time, polygonal walls, and boundaries entwined with climbing plants flash before my eyes through the camera's lens: the Monastery of Sant'Agata, the Roman cisterns and pre-Roman enclosures, the maritime burial ground, the Mithraeum, the two Mausoleums of Lucius Atratinus and Munatius Plancus, and then the Via delle Vignole, the areas of Longato, Casalarga, Monte Cristo, the Colle, the Canals. These are not just places from my childhood, but also repositories of the city's memory, its traditions, and its very history, provided we consider them as urbanized areas since antiquity and increasingly inhabited through settlements, hillside channels, and military roads that were traversed in Roman and medieval times.

The areas and monuments in these zones that are being reclaimed are incredibly vast, rich in additional sources for documentary, on-site, and archival research. These sources are invaluable for certifying, rediscovering, and reevaluating with fresh cultural awareness what this territory has produced over time. However, this can only be achieved if it is approached with the care and attention that its antiquity demands, understanding that the methods used in its construction and production in the past are no longer reproducible or applicable in modern contexts.

One section of this work is titled *Finding in Seeking*, a somewhat intricate and challenging expression that, nevertheless, perfectly encapsulates what is written here: it's not just about finding what one searches for, but also capturing its essence. The act of seeking is the ultimate purpose of one's place in the human dimension (whether in a physical territory or in the realm of philosophical discourse, which, after all, isn't so distant or off-course). Seeking the history of Gaeta means finding something that allows us to recognize and question ourselves, seeking others and the other. Massimo Cacciari, in *L'Arcipelago* (Milan, Adelphi, 1997), wrote that arranging oneself within a hierarchically ordered space is the most effective way to perpetually decline towards one's end. Mutatis mutandis, isolating oneself in ahistorical solutions (or worse, antihistorical ones, as per our discussion) is the most effective way to cut oneself off from novelty and memory. The former is a sign of modernity and the future, while the latter serves as their guarantor. Without one or the other, we reduce ourselves to the status of isolated islands, incapable of recognizing life beyond our own confines.

Finding what is continuously sought is a means of not aging, not withering away in the folds of time that flows despite us. I find it indicative that the pages related to *Finding in Seeking* are dedicated to the industrial ruins of the former ENI refinery, as they preserve the memory of a time rooted in agriculture and medieval traditions, a time dictated and regulated by the labor and prayers, first of monks, and later of peasants. They also encapsulate the novelty of progress, which today, unfortunately, remains in a state of inertia and unusable past, a past that cannot even be dismantled without incurring incalculable damages.

Nevertheless, the photos collected here demonstrate that an invincible, enduring narrative emanates from these ruins, a narrative still capable of speaking from its stone foundations. An almost desperate plea resonates from the images and seems to affect those who gaze upon them. Simultaneously, the written word, being equally entranced by the images, should not be omitted, separated, or relegated to mere captions. Instead, it is the text, skillfully and profoundly influenced by the author, that assumes the crucial role of leading the reader towards the photographs. It separates itself from the play of references and memories with his own recollections and impressions. In doing so, it allows every reader to engage with the text based on their convictions, choices, and ideas while acknowledging the evocative power and ultimate necessity of revisiting oneself, grappling with personal memory and memories, and ultimately constructing a collective memory that empowers rather than erases.

Cles (TN) March 7, 2019
Gennaro Tallini, Università di Verona

01 | The Maritime Burial Ground

Located on the eastern coast and adjacent to the Caboto promenade, remnants of the monument include its base with a semi-subterranean space and parts of the cell walls, partially preserved due to the buildings that have emerged around it in recent years.

According to the writings of Father Lidio Borgese, the archaeologist Amedeo Maiuri believed this could be the actual tomb of Cicero.[1] However, this assertion was discredited by archaeologist Marisa de' Spagnolis, who attributes the burial ground to the Hadrianic period (2nd century AD).

Another hypothesis suggests that the tomb could be the final resting place of Scipio Africanus. According to Cicero and Plutarch, Scipio had a, "passionate interest in collecting seashells and sea stones",[2] right in Gaeta where he had his marble tomb constructed. Supporting this claim, near the tomb there was a votive shrine and a small adjacent space covered with "beautiful red-colored seashells"[3].

To truly unravel the mystery, one would require a discovery of epic proportions, or better yet, a time machine. Who's ready to take on this challenge?

[1] Don Lidio Borgese, *Cajeta Latii Urbs*, Abbazia di Cassino, Cassino, 1966, p. 21.

[2] Scaevol. Ap. Cic., De Or, II, 37; Plutarch., In vit. Scip., in fin. in Nicola Corcia, *Storia delle Due Sicilie dall'antichità più remota al 1789, Volume 1*, Tipografia Virgilio, Naples, 1843.

[3] Pasquale Fantasia, *La rete stradale dell'antica Roma nell'Agro di Gaeta e gli avanzi delle vecchie costruzioni romane nelle sue adiacenze*, Introduzione, Rome, 1947.

This photo manipulation depicts the structure as it might have appeared in the past, before being "engulfed" by modern buildings.
The façade is defined by squared masonry marked by a base and a continuous molding above the entrance's lintel. The vaulted ceiling that covers the building is constructed with uncertain masonry. The small window has been "removed," as it seems to be a later addition.

Searching for the Keys

In search of the key,
In a pocket, a drawer,
Within our own being;

Unlocking the gate at last,
The unfamiliar, our air to breathe.

We are seekers
Before being human.

The ground level outside the site has certainly expanded
for clear urban reasons; the molded horizontal surface
that serves as an architrave is particularly notable.

The Roman structure is suffocated by invasive plants and surrounded by crops. In any case, the exterior wall is the result of a medieval alteration of the site, aiming to reconstruct a collapsed area. The current entrance to the sacred area should emphasize the ancient entrance, positioned discreetly to better conceal the initiatory rituals from the outside.

02 | The Mithraeum

The Mithraeum of Gaeta, even if only for a few meters, considering its location at the slopes of Mount Cefalo, in the area of San Giacomo, was a zone traditionally cultivated by farmers from Itri. It's a matter of municipal boundaries, which are shifted a few meters every century or so. These few meters, however, render the Mithraeum yet another hidden treasure in Gaeta.

The Mithraeum was a place of worship dedicated to the god Mithras, a deity with origins in Hinduism and Persia, but also influenced by Hellenistic and Roman cultures. It was revered in esoteric religions from the 1st century BC to the 5th century AD.

It's intriguing to think that Mithraism came very close to becoming the dominant religion of our time. It had spread throughout every province of the Roman Empire, to the point where some emperors adopted it as the official religion. Christianity only narrowly surpassed it. Nevertheless, not all was lost, and as with other "pagan" cults, various elements of Mithraism merged into Christianity.

The worship of Mithras took place in enclosed and usually hidden locations, designed to evoke the rock from which the god was believed to have been born. Following tradition, the Mithraeum of Gaeta isn't immediately visible, but concealed within the remnants of a Roman villa dating back to the 1st century BC, specifically within its cryptoporticus.

The Mithraeum of Gaeta boasts a rectangular layout with a barrel vault, featuring two masonry benches where devotees could offer their prayers. Inside these benches, there are seven small niches, symbolizing seven stages of purification and initiation into the cult.

For the local farmers, this place full of charm and mystery has always been known as "The Caves." Who knows if, upon entering, someone among them has ever faintly sensed the ancient litanies that once filled the silence of the small temple?

The Eternal Alliance

Your very name signifies an alliance, the everlasting friendship that the people of this land once pledged to you, only to betray as circumstances changed. History is written by the victors, and the same applies to religions: everything passes, even today. Seeing your ancient temple in ruins, I can't help but travel by imagination to an era when it played a prominent spiritual role. From the fog of the past, weathered-faced peasants and passing travelers reemerge. They perform gestures, then enter the small temple with an air of reverence, bowing before your idol and offering something as tribute. Each gives what they can. A birth is celebrated, a bountiful harvest, a departed loved one is commemorated... Are you truly so different from the gods we have today and those we will have tomorrow? You won't truly vanish as long as humanity endures, with its questions, fears, and triumphs.

So don't hold it against us for the ruin of your earthly abode. Up there, amidst the stars, you will always have your true home: the yearning of humankind to unite with the divine.

The worship hall is outlined by a façade with a niche that was once adorned with polychrome marbles; the channels for water flow are still visible, which, through gravity, reached the sacrificial basin at the center of the space. The rough work on the walls and the imprint of the arch under the barrel vault are clearly visible. Subsequent uses after the suppression of the cult have partly obscured the ancient splendor, but some elements of refinement attributed to the Mithraic worship can still be identified.

03 | The Monastery of Colle Sant'Agata

The Monastery of Colle Sant'Agata was built by the will of Bishop Francesco Gattola in 1327 with the purpose of accommodating a group of hermits from the Third Franciscan Order,[1] gaining significant importance in the ecclesiastical hierarchy of Gaeta over the centuries. Its religious history came to an end in the mid-eighteenth century when it was abandoned, a fate shared by the nearby Monastery of Santo Spirito di Zannone.

During the siege of Gaeta by the Napoleonic Empire in 1806, the *cenobium* of the monastery served as a refuge for the loyalist group led by Colonel Michele Pezza (Fra' Diavolo) of the Kingdom of Naples. From 1836, during the devastating cholera epidemic that struck the city, the monastery first served as a lazzaretto, and then as a burial place for the friars and the people of Gaeta themselves, leading to it becoming the subject of supernatural tales in the subsequent years.

Its position atop Colle Sant'Agata allows the monastery to dominate the entire surrounding territory and a considerable stretch of the coastline. The Piedmontese army recognized its strategic importance during the siege of 1860-61, when they built a battery there; however, it remained unused and was quickly abandoned.

The military history of the former monastery didn't end there: the Italian Navy used it as a guard post during World War I to spot potential incursions by Austrian and German ships. However, during World War II, the bombings that devastated the area spared not even the old monastery: the Allies, mistaking it for a Nazi position, fired an artillery shell against it, destroying the bell tower in one fell swoop.

[1] Since 1978 known as the Secular Franciscan Order, it is composed of Christians who commit to living the Gospel in the manner of St. Francis of Assisi, within their secular state, and observing a specific rule approved by the Church.

Until the early 1970s, on the afternoons of October 31st, November 1st, and 2nd, a ritual was held at the monastery to commemorate the victims of cholera. Around the same period, the Gaeta Boy Scout troop removed the old bones from the monastery's cisterns, exposing them to anyone visiting before giving them a new and proper burial.

The structure, currently privately owned, is surrounded by a network of barbed wire that seems to date back to the 1970s. Just beyond the barbed wire, a series of monoliths (perhaps placed there by the Auruncan people?) appears to encircle the monastery in what must have been a protective barrier against external threats.

Today, the monastery stands in the state of abandonment visible in the photos. This state, far from diminishing its charm, contributes to its poignant beauty.

At the hill's summit, imposing façades of the structure rise, along with sections of vaults that still maintain their balance, defying gravitational forces, overgrown vegetation, and structural instabilities.

The cloister, largely collapsed, was structured with four wings supported by pilasters and cross-vaults arranged five on each side. The square cloister is outlined by a portico upheld by elegant, spacious pillars made of blocks and masonry, which in turn support the vaults. The Gothic lines are distinct, accentuated by a series of ribs that lighten the arches' form.

On the next page, the drone image provides a comprehensive view of the entire complex, situated at the hill's summit. It offers a holistic perspective of the site and of the space that unfolds around the cloister.

The only remaining wing of the cloister: the floor is obscured by thick layers of collapsed debris and overgrown vegetation.

*The underlying cistern has been breached at multiple
points to facilitate the burial of cholera victims.*

Hostel of Souls

The view from up here is truly fantastic, so breathtaking that someone would like to turn this place into a hotel. I hold no bias against the conservation of historically and artistically significant places by the private sector, as long as it's done according to precise rules aimed at restoring and promoting the site. When I was a child, near the Calegna overpass, a commercial space was built where there once stood a well-preserved Roman arch. After its construction, mysteriously, the arch disappeared. I hope it was relocated somewhere with the coordination of the Superintendent's Office rather than being destroyed and discarded.

In essence, the Monastery of Sant'Agata could possibly become a hotel in the future. I like to think that even today, it welcomes the few visitors who, enamored by its beauty and tranquility, pause to contemplate the landscape below and imagine the place as it was in a distant past. An inn for souls, where no entry fee is paid, with one rule alone: leave everything as you find it, as if you were an ethereal being drifting above the ruins.

The sparse fragments of frescoes still in place are evidence of a cultural vibrancy and the esteem with which this location was held. Only a few images remain visible; notably, a pope is depicted, adorned in sacred vestments and a tiara, although his identity is difficult to discern.

Ruins of Saint Agatha

No longer does the crowd ascend, on feast days,
to refresh themselves at your polluted altar,
nor do the poor stop at your threshold anymore,
with a bowl for their meal.

The diligent housewife used to open the door,
as soon as she heard the friar's knocking:
"Deo gratias!" while to her, with bare head bowed,
the devout one said: "May God give

generous recompense!" Now you lie
in the squalor of abandonment, and the
beauty they have taken from you, rapacious hands.

And naked, skeletal, no longer the one
who lived the splendor of vibrant years,
by ravens and serpents, you are a consumed dwelling.

Don Salvatore Buonomo

04 | The Monastery of Santo Spirito of Zannone in Gaeta

The island of Zannone belongs to the Pontine Archipelago and is located about 6 km from Ponza. Zannone, formerly known as "Sinonia" (Σηνωνία in Ancient Greek), hosted a Benedictine monastic community until 813, when the monks abandoned the island due to Saracen raids.

In 1213, some monks of the same Order from Sant'Angelo of Gaeta returned to the island and began to observe the Rule of Joachim of Fiore. In 1237, they requested to become part of the Cistercian Order, and by 1246, upon the request of Pope Innocent IV, the monastery became a Cistercian abbey under the name of Santo Spirito of Zannone.

Image courtesy of Google Maps. The complex is nestled among the ENI storage tanks. The masses of masonry and enclosing wall are clearly visible from above. Notably, the surrounding conduits are designed to divert around the medieval architecture to avoid "polluting" or damaging it.

However, the presence of the Cistercians on the island was not destined to last: in 1291, much like the Benedictines centuries before, the community sought to relocate to the mainland due to ongoing Saracen incursions.

The abbots of Fossanova, Casamari, and the island monastery decided that the monks would settle in the fertile plain of Arzano in Gaeta. This is believed to have taken place under the leadership of Abbot Goffredo around 1295, as indicated by the date on the entrance arch of the monastery.

The inscription on the arch is associated with a historical anachronism: although the monastery was built during the papacy of Boniface VIII (the 193rd pope), the monks deliberately omitted his name and that of his predecessor, Celestine V (the 192nd pope, famously known as the Pope of Dante's "Great Refusal"), in favor of Nicholas IV (the 191st pope), who had already been deceased for three years at the time. To further confirm that this error was intentional, the inscription correctly identifies the reigning monarch of the time, Charles II of Anjou.

Detail of the monumental portal of the church, created with modulated blocks that support the architrave bearing the inscription:

✟ ANNO · DNI · M · CC · NONAG · QUINTO · FUNDATU · FUIT · ISTUD · MONAS /
TERIUM · ABABATE · GUTTIFRIDO · ADHONOREM · SRS · SCI · BEATE · / MARIE
· SEMP · VIRGIS · ET BEATI · IOHIS · EVANGLIST · TERE · DNI · NICOLAI / PP · IIII ·
ETREGIS · KAROLI · II · HOC · OP · FIEI · FEC · PETR · ORAINEIO · PMICI · GAGET ·

Photo kindly provided by Carlo Di Nitto (1973).

The monastery follows the Gothic style favored by the Cistercians and was constructed on the remains of a previous Roman building. It was dedicated to the Holy Spirit, the Virgin Mary, and St. John the Evangelist. Active until 1750, when it was abandoned, the monastery is now enclosed within the former ENI refinery and is not normally accessible for visits.

***

"I saw and recognized the shade of him
who due to cowardice made the great refusal."
—*Inferno*, Canto III, 59–60

Dante famously assigns blame to Celestine V for the unexpected ascent of Boniface VIII to the papal throne, yet the historical narrative behind this event is – as it always is for historic events – more intricate. In truth, Celestine V, previously a hermit known as Pietro di Morrone, did reluctantly assume the papal role, serving from his election on July 5, 1294 (he was already 79 years old), until his resignation on December 13, 1294.

Pope Celestine V soon recognized his limitations in wielding authority and his unsuitability for the demands of papal responsibilities, particularly given his lack of political acumen. We can't help but wonder, why was a hermit chosen as pope in the first place? The Conclave had grappled with the inability to select a pope for two years due to competing factions vying for power. Pietro di Morrone, who was by then a well-known holy man, sent a letter warning the cardinals that God was unhappy with the power-struggle tearing apart the church. Upon reading this plea, Latino Malabranca, the aged Dean of the College of Cardinals, famously exclaimed, "In the name of the Father, the Son, and the Holy Spirit, I elect Brother Pietro di Morrone!" The cardinals swiftly ratified Malabranca's desperate decision. When summoned, Pietro adamantly resisted accepting the papacy and, as Petrarch recounts, even attempted to flee until he was ultimately persuaded by a delegation of cardinals, accompanied by the king of Naples and the claimant to the Hungarian throne, Charles Martel of Anjou. Pietro di Morrone – now Celestine V – would soon come to regret writing that letter, but this story is for another time...

Finding in Seeking

"Those gray and imposing walls, those arches… it was a split second: they were there, waiting for me for centuries".[1]

Today, the church stands significantly devastated by several collapses. The taste for the Gothic style is evident in the triumphal arch and the portal. Just outside the entrance, slightly off-center, stands the bell tower, with a dovecote perched on top.

As a child, I used to make my way from Via Indipendenza up to Monte Tortona to visit my grandparents. It was quite a trek! But I preferred saving my money for a comic book or a round at the video game arcade, rather than spending it on the bus fare. Looking out towards the sea from Monte Tortona, you can see half of the gulf. It truly is a shame that enormous, rusted cisterns and towering chimneys mar the beauty of

[1] Jason R. Forbus, *Trovare il Cercare in Storie d'Oltredove*, Ali Ribelli Edizioni, Gaeta, 2016

the landscape. Indeed, it took me years to take notice of the ancient ruins of the Santo Spirito di Zannone Monastery amidst the colossal remnants of an industrial past that, though short-lived, left many scars on Gaeta's beauty.

It wasn't until I was fifteen that I mustered the audacity (yes, even at that young age!) to walk to the town hall on my own and inquire about those mysterious and fascinating ruins. Under cover of night, without my older brother knowing, I used his computer to write what would become my first short story – *Finding in Seeking* – in which I recounted the extraordinary tale of the monastery and its current state of abandonment in the fantastical manner that characterizes everything I write. I tried my luck and submitted the story to a national contest (the Premio Campiello Giovani), and imagine my surprise when I found out I had become a national finalist and secured first place in the Lazio region!

Only the presbyterial area is still covered by a cross-vault, which stands out from the well-defined piers in the masonry.

In Latina, the politicians and journalists who attended the award ceremony couldn't believe that Gaeta harbored a monastery of such vast dimensions and with such a fascinating history, tucked away among dismal fuel tanks, mostly abandoned for years. Unknowingly, I was becoming a spokesperson for a part of Gaeta's illustrious history that, due to negligence and unfortunate historical circumstances, had fallen into oblivion.

Many years later, in 2010, thanks to then-City Councillor for State Property Antonio Ciano, I managed to obtain permission from ENI to visit the monastery. The photos taken on that occasion are an extraordinary testament to the glorious past of our city that, I hope, will emerge from obscurity to once again become part of Gaeta's archaeological heritage.

In the cloister are present various rooms, including the Chapter Hall, whose entrance and two small windows are adorned with brickwork decorations.

From the outside, the well-defined polygonal masonry boundary is clearly visible, dating back centuries before the construction of the monastery complex—a clear indication of its Roman antecedents.

The entrance to the complex appears quite simple in form and architectural technique, while the church portal boasts its own monumentality thanks to the moldings and materials used.

... of Gaeta dates back to the period of the city's greatest prestige, during the rule of the Docibile dynasty. Gaeta flourished and grew under their reign, becoming a significant maritime power in all respects. The palace was commissioned by John I (882-933 AD) and was located in what is now Piazza dei Commestibili in medieval Gaeta. It stands as a tangible testament to an era when the city expanded its trade across the Mediterranean and beyond, minted its own coin (the *follaro*), and strategically wielded both arms and diplomacy to its advantage.

It's worth considering how this glorious history can be revitalized and structured to serve as a cultural and tourist attraction for our city.

The tower is supported by large blocks arranged in a square formation, later reassembled with the addition of mortar and brick and limestone wedges.

The inscription on the tower identifies the patronage of the imperial patrician John, son of Duke Docibile.

The Ducal Palace of Gaeta

In days of yore, a noble sire did rise,
A palace tall he built, with soaring skies,
To reign o'er sea and reach celestial might,
His dreams held aloft in wondrous flight.

But now, it lies in disarray
Its ruins a whisper of bygone days
A distant memory of its grand design,
Lost to the ages, a legacy's decline.

Only his name endures, a silent roar,
Within the lion's mouth, forevermore.

The lion in the center of the square has often raised doubts about the square's name.

*At the base of the tower, a massive Roman frieze is incorporated into
the wall, adorned with a series of reliefs depicting scenes of navigation
and fishing, interspersed with depictions of fish and sea creatures.*

*Stone and marble make up the tower's soaring masonry, taken and reused from
demolished Roman structures. The square holes in the large blocks bear evidence
of a wooden structure that once adorned the exterior of the Ducal Palace.*

The house of Sebastiano Conca (Gaeta, January 8, 1680 – Gaeta, September 1, 1764),[1] an illustrious citizen of Gaeta whose artwork is exhibited in major museums both worldwide and in Gaeta itself, is a hidden treasure that deserves to be included in guided tours.

The house presents itself as an exquisite rural dwelling, featuring a small yet elegant portico with arches, a ground floor with small rooms (now used for agricultural storage), an upper floor serving as a summer residence for a private individual, and a small terrace.

At one time, one of the small rooms on the ground floor served as a private chapel, and in the early 20th century, the walls still bore partial frescoes, most likely painted by Conca's own students. Regrettably, the remnants of these frescoes were concealed under a layer of lime to make way for a pigsty.

The entire Monte a Mare where Conca's house is located, despite its proximity to Sant'Agostino Beach, still maintains a largely agricultural character, although some plots of land have been overrun by brambles. There are also several villas and cottages, some of which can be attributed to wealthy – through not necessarily reputable – individuals.

[1] "Sebastiano Conca most likely died in Gaeta rather than Naples, as previously believed. In 1764, a cholera epidemic erupted following the severe agricultural famine that afflicted the Kingdom of Naples and its capital in 1763 and 1764 (as reported by Antonio Cervone in the Gazzetta di Gaeta, 1980, II, 17). It is probable that Conca's remains were interred in the Annunziata not only due to the artist's social status but also that of his family. "Some documents related to the artistic and engraving activities of his brother Giovanni are detailed in *La collezione Giustiniani: Inventari I-Inventari II*, edited by Silvia Danesi Squarzina (Turin, Einaudi, 2011). An indispensable chapter in Sebastiano's biography and bibliography can be found in *Sebastiano Conca, catalogo della mostra*, edited by O. Michel, Gaeta, La Poligrafica, 1981. For further information on this matter, also refer to my contribution in *Civilta Aurunca*, 36, 1997, pp. 16-42, which discusses a nearly unknown painting by Sebastiano Conca. In this article, I highlighted the discovery of a painting by the Gaetan artist in a church in Ardenno (SO), a piece not documented in any catalog." – Gennaro Tallini

The dwelling, notably massive in size, features an oversized masonry structure. This is due to its construction as a standalone building in an extra-urban area. Currently, it displays several filled-in arches, which were added to close off a section of the porch.

This drone image reveals the symmetry of the building through its volumes, arches, and windows.

*Sebastiano Conca's painting "The Patron Saints Erasmo and Marciano
Blessing the City of Gaeta," created in 1749, captures a moment of significance.
The artwork was commissioned to adorn the council chamber of Gaeta's
Municipality. Alongside the depictions of the patrons, the urban settlement, its
layout, walls, and Mount Orlando are all depicted from an aerial perspective.
The artist's evolution is evident as he initially mistakenly portrays the Alfonsina
Tower of the Aragonese Castle at an exaggerated size, but he later revises this
depiction. The Municipality of Gaeta allocated 50 ducats for the creation of this
painting, reflecting its value and importance in the local public sphere on May 5, 1749.*

There is a distinct transition in the building's masonry, with limestone used for the lower sections and tuff for the upper portions. The remnants of a wine press's foundation harken back to the cultivation of vines, a practice replaced by olive cultivation in the latter half of the previous century.

The sunset of Sebastiano

Naples, September 1st, 1764

The bedroom lies in shadow, with only a sliver of light cutting across the floor, venturing toward a desk at its feet. On the desk rests a small mountain of papers, many of them scrawled with doodles, fragments of masterpieces in patient anticipation.

But the creator sleeps, showing no sign of waking. Weary under the weight of years, he lies in a bed that grows ever larger and more unwelcoming

"Sir, wake up... Sir..."

A voice and a hand reach to torment him, compelling him to open his eyes. It's Placido, the exuberant Sicilian apprentice, one foot in the world of art and the other in the elite circles of Naples. The young man understands that an artist thrives not just on canvases, but on bows, greetings, and connections. The kind that can secure significant commissions, like frescoing the interior of a basilica or painting a noble's portrait.

"Sir, Monsignor Mauri has confirmed the appointment for today. And the Duchess of Parma, visiting the Prince of Torre Annunziata, would like to meet you. I believe it's for a portrait. And then there's the matter of the Sanctuary of Pozzano, and..."

"Water," he managed to utter, chasing the words like an oasis in the desert.

"Water," Placido repeated dumbfoundedly, then quickly left the room, returning moments later with a pitcher and a cup.

"Drink, Sir, and forgive me for waking you, but the preparations for numerous and noble guests are many and..."

With a wave of his hand, the master gestured that it didn't matter, impossible to discern whether he referred to the offense of the abrupt awakening or the many noble guests about to assail his day.

He took the cup offered, finishing it in two long sips, then invited Placido to pour more water, and the crystalline sound of the liquid seemed the most beautiful melody he had ever heard.

"He's quite thirsty this morning..."

The master wiped his beard of the water droplets that adorned it. He pushed back the sheets and placed his first foot on the floor. The effort elicited a sigh. Placido promptly offered his arm, aiding him in pulling himself up.

The day stretched out interminably, and not just because of the many and unwanted guests—men and women who were anything but interested in art. What they craved was a name, his name; obtaining a work by Sebastiano Conca, regardless of its scale or subject, would confer prestige upon their respective families.

Throughout his over fifty-year career, he had worked for Popes, Princes, and Princesses. His skill

had earned him the title of "Cavaliere," a title he hadn't hesitated to exploit in a different phase of his life to open doors. Always, it was said, in the name of art, to carve out spaces necessary for experimentation.

It had all been in pursuit of vanity – the lavish Naples apartment, the refined clothing. With the wisdom of age, he now understood.

That was a closed chapter. Something within him had changed. It had been changing for a few days now, but today he sensed a definitive rupture, the exact same sensation that had driven him to abandon works otherwise finished in the past.

There was a peculiar weariness in him, not just in his limbs but for things themselves. The walls of the room felt like prison walls. The journey from the bedroom to the dining hall seemed endless and tedious. Things didn't improve during breakfast—hardly any food touched his lips. Once in his studio, he barely glanced at his last two finished paintings, one of which had already been purchased by the Spanish Royals, a Madonna with Child that radiated the Rococo light that had characterized his recent years in Naples.

"Sir, I wish to show you my latest work: a Magdalene in the likeness of our skilled cook, Francesca."

The elderly master looked at the painting: masterfully executed, undoubtedly worthy of admiration under different circumstances.

"Superb work, no doubt," he said, running his fingers along the edges of the canvas. "Your apprenticeship ends today."

Those long-awaited words staggered Placido: "Sir, you honor me greatly..."

"None of that. If I recall correctly, you wish to return to Sicily. I'll write a letter to some of my acquaintances on your behalf. This way, you'll have work upon your arrival."

"Thank you very much, Sir!"

"And just stop calling me 'Sir': the word is old, perhaps older than me. Send word to our illustrious guests that I will receive them this afternoon at four."

Still reeling from the news, Placido bid farewell to the master and hurried away, entrusting two servants with the task of delivering the message. He himself headed to the Duchess, a woman renowned for her beauty.

Finally alone, Sebastiano first wrote three letters, more or less the same but addressed to different people—distinguished Sicilians who would help Placido establish himself. Then, relieved of other duties, he sank into the chair where he often sat in contemplation between works, and where he had conceived some of his finest pieces.

He closed his eyes, ready to embrace the bustling world of his memories. Strangely, he didn't see any of the characters, big or small, he had encountered over the course of his long life. No castle, church, or palace opened their doors to him. None of that.

What he saw was a road: narrow and dirt-packed, winding its way up the crest of a hill. Halfway up stood a charming house, so distant from the opulence in which he had lived. That was his ancestral home, where he was born and raised. He saw himself as a child, descending the hill toward the lush oak forest just to the north. There, he loved to spend the extended moments of dreams, sketching the outlines of waves, seagulls, distant fishing boats on the sand... Thus, he passed the time, or perhaps time passed through him.

On a particularly inspired morning, young Sebastiano had gone beyond his usual sketches. Armed with natural pigments to color the sand, he was determined to create an actual "painting." He didn't yet know what he would depict, but he was adamant about doing it. A promising step for any aspiring artist.

First, he mixed sand and the pigments to create various colors: white, yellow, orange, red, purple, blue, black. But what to depict? Lost in thought, he looked down at the sand and saw bare feet approaching: it was a woman, beautiful and somewhat wild, with impossibly long black hair, emerald green eyes, and a complexion pale as the moon. She wore a long midnight blue dress, rather tattered. She must have come from the sea, as both her hair and dress dripped with water. Despite her somewhat disheveled appearance, she carried a strange aura that made Sebastiano rise to his feet, his fists still clutching the sand that slid slowly between his fingers, recreating the eternal flow of time.

The woman stopped a certain distance away and watched him. Sebastiano couldn't say how much time passed, but after a while, as he looked at the ground, he realized he had completed his portrait: it was her, the woman, looking at him with an extraordinary intensity through two incandescent sand eyes.

By the time he raised his gaze, the lady had vanished. There were footprints leading slowly into the

woods. Sebastiano followed them, not understanding why, but feeling drawn by the inevitable call of destiny.

He arrived before five intertwined oaks, shaped by human hands into a welcoming hut. After a moment of hesitation, Sebastiano crossed the slightly-ajar door.

Inside, in the semi-darkness of her bedroom, he saw himself—old and minuscule—lying on the expansive canopy bed that had borne witness to his mortal glory. There was Placido, and the Monsignor, and the Duchess of Parma, and other faces he couldn't distinguish in the shadows. But most importantly, at the corner of the room, unseen by anyone else, was her. Unchanged, with a pool of water at her feet that, drop by drop, grew larger.

"You've returned," she said to him, smiling a strange and melancholic smile.

"Yes," the boy replied, accepting the soft, damp hand she extended, a hand that had touched him once before, at the beginning of his journey.

"Come, I'll show you the treasure I spoke of that day."

The room's door swung open, revealing a sunset of extraordinary beauty: the sun descending slowly into the sea, streaking the sky with a thousand colors, creating marvelous plays of light among the sandy dunes.

This was the beach of his youth, where he'd collected dreams like seashells and built, grain by grain, the castle of his life. A life that was now flowing away like sand slipping through his fingers, returning to the greatest treasure of creation.

Sebastiano closed his eyes, letting himself be carried away by the infinite.

And he became the wealthiest of men.

Dedicated to Sebastiano Conca, an illustrious painter from Gaeta, whose house can still be seen today on the hill overlooking the Sant'Agostino Beach.

07 | The Church of Sant'Angelo dei Marzi and the Roman Structure

Not far from the ancient Appian Way and near the "Venticinque Ponti" train overpass, heading towards Itri along the seaside, down a country road and across a Roman bridge, you arrive at the Church of Sant'Angelo dei Marzi.[1]

[1] "The church is mentioned in the *Statuta, Privilegia et Consuetudines Civitatis Caietae* (Chapter CCXXXII, c. 39r, 1553). It had the right to have a juror, just like the Formian fractions of Castellione and Mola, plagia Sant'Andrea (now Piaja), burgo Sancti Cosme, All'arco in Sancto Sergio (current parish of San Giacomo), Tesa (Annunziata area), and

The single-nave building is constructed on the edge of the Pontone stream, along the same axis. The layout is organized into three bays. Today, the presbyterial area is separated by a later-added wall, which likely preserved its corresponding roofing.

The first documentary evidence of the site is found within a papal bull issued by Pope Adrian IV in the year 1158. The peculiar title *de martiis*, which lacks similar cases in the territory, is explained in the *Codex Diplomaticus Cajetanus* "as the intention to connect the church to the worship of Saint Gabriel, whose celebrations were held at the end of the month of March".[2] Among the ancient little churches scattered throughout the Gaetan territory, this one, despite its abandonment, still displays frescoes, albeit significantly deteriorated.

Costanbersa along the Annunziata road leading to the former tennis club. The lands in the area where the church stands were mostly owned by families residing in burgo Sancti Cosme. Around the year 997 or perhaps in 1011, Bishop Bernardo expelled the priest and primicerio Leone and his son from those properties for refusing to carry out necessary repairs. He replaced them in the administration of the ruined church of Sancti Cosme et Damiani and the related uncultivated land with a priest and two canons from Rome. He granted them full jurisdictional freedom and the right to use, possess, care for, improve, officiate, and bequeath the religious building along with all courtyards, lands, and locations. One of the two canons, Benedetto, belonged to the Roman Marzi family, from which the interesting toponymy of the area (sant'Agnolo) likely originated, as well as the dedication of the building (notes by Cosimo Di Russo on the website http://www.telefree.it/news.php?op=view&id=105938)." – Gennaro Tallini.
[2] C.D.C, III, p. 283.

On the adjacent page, the structurally best-preserved area is the
presbytery, where a moderately visible cycle of frescoes with a series
of saints and evangelists on two superimposed registers remains.
These frescoes can be dated back to the early 14th century.

The church today is located below the level of the road. The main
portal is distinguished by molded stone blocks and features a lunette
where traces of a lost fresco's sinopia can still be discerned.

I mentioned a Roman bridge, yet I omitted to highlight that, due to its proximity to the ancient Appian Way, the area is quite archaeologically rich. Scattered across the countryside are visible remains of structures dating back to the Roman period, including, right in front of the small church, what appears to be a majestic edifice.

Upon closer inspection, it becomes evident that several of the stones comprising the church walls exhibit craftsmanship repurposed from a nearby structure as spolia.

The concern is that this spoliation might continue today, as these sites are abandoned and located in sparsely-frequented areas. This might encourage potential wrongdoers to detach a piece here and another there, perhaps to give an antique touch to their villa, thereby depriving the entire community and future generations of the opportunity to experience the allure of a history that still has much to reveal.

The Roman bridge rests upon large blocks and extends across a conglomerate with uncertain workmanship; the arches exhibit a significantly lowered profile. The use of reinforced concrete and iron beams above appears in stark contrast.

A block of the external facing in squared masonry.

Sant'Angelo dei Marzi

Draped in ancient stones so finely arrayed,
Yet, upon close inspection's steady gaze,
You stand, unaltered, a familiar tomb's embrace.
I touch your walls, in search of hands concealed,
That fashioned you, their art in stone revealed.

From art to monument, your essence blooms,
A timeless legacy in seasons' endless rooms.
Unveiling and dressing with each passing day,
Through the world's ever-changing, rhythmic play.

Near the church, a Roman structure built of brick masonry and an unknown secondary material is quite evident. It remarkably preserves its vaults almost entirely intact.

Growing up in Gaeta between the 1980s and 1990s – time sure flies! – was like living out the cult film *The Goonies*,[1] in which a group of adventurous kids go through numerous escapades to… discover a treasure! And in those days, Gaeta, for us young explorers, was indeed a vast island filled with treasures waiting to be unearthed.

The area of Calegna was a particular haunt of ours: rising next to the now-demolished American School of Gaeta, the multi-billion-Lira Tribunal construction site was, for us, a massive playground. Behind easily surmounted fences and gates, we found a world of untouched construction materials, bags of cement, and bricks that were like life-sized Lego. But, most importantly, Calegna was the place from which you could (and still can) easily access one of the most picturesque sections of Gaeta's railway.

As we walked beside its hushed, tranquil railway tracks, we found ourselves crossing a seemingly endless, dimly lit, and eerie tunnel. In those days, it was a favored haunt for gatherings of misguided individuals who fancied themselves as devil-worshipers. In this desolate place, they subjected unfortunate animals to torture and ignited pyres of olive branches, adding an unsettling aura to the surroundings. Our vivid imaginations led us to distinctly hear the whistle of an approaching phantom train. How can we ever forget the almond tree standing by the tracks? We used to climb it, reaching its peak to savor almonds, carefully discarding those infested by worms. From that lofty perch, we gazed down upon the Calegna valley and stretched our sight further, taking in the majestic Gulf that unfolded before our eyes…

[1] *The Goonies* is an adventure film from 1985 directed by Richard Donner. The screenplay by Chris Columbus was adapted from a story by Steven Spielberg, who also produced the film.

The day before this writing, after many years, I revisited that place. It remained unchanged, or nearly so, with perhaps a few additional cracks in the small cabin. The railway crossroad appeared somewhat somber and forlorn, leaving me to wonder if, just maybe, we had been missed there, even if only a little.

Today, I've heard discussions about the restoration of the "Littorina" train, and that news fills me with great joy, as it promises to bring immense benefits to the entire community. Yet, deep within my heart, a touch of sadness lingers at the prospect of bidding farewell to this ethereal landscape.

As they say, "Beauty is in the eyes of the beholder." I'd like to add to that bit of wisdom that true beauty resides not only in what we see, but also in the youthful hearts that appreciate it and in those irreplaceable moments that mean the entire world to those who live them fully.

The Train of Memories

Your final echo softly sighs,
Train of memories, under distant skies,
Step down at the station's call,
A new path awaits, beyond it all:
Forward you go, a single track,
Toward the horizon, and never back,
Journey's end, all tales are told,
Fading away, you once were gold.

The ruined hut at the level crossing is almost like a commemorative monument of a completely vanished work.

The viaduct of the "Twenty-five Bridges", almost completely rebuilt after World War II, has once again welcomed the tracks of the "Littorina" train.

09 | The Caves of Sant'Agostino

Wealthy Romans were renowned for their extravagant and stylish way of life. Although some of their culinary practices and customs might appear peculiar to us in the 21st century – such as the use of *garum*[1] – one undeniable fact remains: they possessed a profound appreciation for the magnificent sea and knew how to luxuriate along its shores. This sentiment is beautifully captured by the numerous ruins of ancient Roman villas that pepper our entire Ulysses Riviera, with some remarkably well-preserved examples. In Gaeta, for instance, the notable remains of the villa belonging to Consul Gnaeus Fonteius from the 1st century BC stand proudly on the stunning Fontania beach.

As it goes, anything that isn't immediately before our eyes runs the risk of fading into obscurity or being known only to a few enthusiasts. The *Grotte di Sant'Agostino*, though among Gaeta's better-known hidden treasures, are no exception.

These caves are, in fact, the remnants of a Roman villa dating back to around the mid-1st century BC to the 2nd century AD, a time of great splendor during the ancient Romans' *Dolce Vita* in our region. The ruins, more commonly referred to as the "Acque Salse," are located at the northern end of the long Sant'Agostino beach.

According to legends, some bandits who once operated in our region used these caves as one of their countless hideouts, concealing the entrance with branches and stones.

"In one cave, they stored provisions, in another, they kept their weapons, and in one with red walls, they slept. Near this, there was one they called *de gliè musecante*,[2] because there were frescoes of

[1] A liquid sauce made from fish innards and salted fish that ancient Romans used as a seasoning for many first and second courses.
[2] "Of the musician" in the Gaetan-Borghiciano (outside the walls) dialect.

musicians on the walls. To eat, so as not to give away their position with the smoke from the fire, they would go to the *ponte de gliu Scarpone* (Scarpone Point) to a place called *la mese de glie bregante* (the bandits' table). For added security, they assigned one of their own to keep a vigilant watch from an excellent vantage point known as *gliu gliene russe* (the red wood)".[3]

It's quite an intriguing twist of fate for a villa that, two thousand years ago, hosted wealthy and influential individuals and their retinues, only to transform into a sanctuary for men and women on the run from the law.

[3] Nicola Magliocca, *Usi e costumi del popolo gaetano*, Centro Storico Culturale, Gaeta, 1994.

The vaulted spaces serve as a foundation for a structure that is now completely lost.

The upper cistern is constructed of uncertain masonry and coated
with cocciopesto *(a type of waterproof plaster made from crushed*
pottery), while the vault is made of conglomerate and was poured over
a centering structure, the imprints of which are clearly visible.

The space is a long corridor, situated in front of the tanks, which could have served as a storage area for various goods.

10 | The Church of Saint Ambrose

You might have seen it a thousand times while traveling from Gaeta to Itri through the Arzano plain: a ruin decidedly more imposing than the many rural structures in the Conca area. Driven by curiosity and the enthusiastic accounts of a couple of friends who had visited the site a few months earlier, I discovered that the ruin is, in fact, what remains of the Church of Sant'Ambrogio: a renowned temple, notable for preserving within its walls the vivid fresco of a crusader knight, or perhaps Saint George, though the image is barely visible now.

After a few days of patient waiting, I finally managed to carve out the first available hour to visit the site. I got into my car and reached the area, where I parked to climb up the steep slope that lead to the ruin.

Initially, I made a wrong turn, and ended up on top of a deserted hill. No big deal: from up there, even though the view was marred by the hideous structures of the former ENI oil refinery, I could still see the sea and Gaeta, dozing off.

I retraced my steps and, this time, took the right path, so that after two hundred meters, I was already close to the ruin.

At this point, I came to realize what had been previously mentioned to me – the ancient little church had been repurposed as a shepherd's dwelling However, I refused to be deterred, and proceeded to ascend the rear of the ruin. There, a natural elevation in the terrain allowed me to reach out and touch the still-intact barrel vault (possibly dating back to the 13th century) of the church and take in the adjacent cistern.

I continued my walk through the bushes, and suddenly, I spotted a magnificent shepherd dog, notably large, which confidently strides my way the moment it catches sight of me. Dogs had never been a source of fear for me, in part because of my experiences as a teenager, when I worked summer jobs distributing flyers. Those jobs often placed me in situations where slipping a flyer into a mailbox meant risking my hand being chomped on by a vigilant guard dog.

*The space is a long corridor, situated in front of the tanks, which
could have served as a storage area for various goods.*

The dog was now quite near, and I found myself standing there,
wearing a somewhat foolish smile on my face, with my hand raised in
a friendly greeting. Luckily, the shepherd appeared, and with a swift
glance, he grasped the situation and assured me that there was no
cause for concern – the dog would only aggressive when provoked.

The dog came closer and, indeed, let itself be petted, quite happy
with the attention.

At this point, I introduced myself to the shepherd, and he carefully
scrutinized me from head to toe. Then, as is common for older people
in our area, he inquired, "Whose son are you?" To which, I hesitantly
explained that my father was an American navy officer stationed in
Gaeta and provide my mother's surname. The shepherd quickly does
the math in his mind and then asks me, "Are you Cicce's grandson?"

And so I came to know that "Cicce" or "Ciccio", as my grandfather Francesco Sinopoli was affectionately known, was, let's say, a friend of the shepherd; they knew each other well. The situation turned around: from being a strange and awkward young man wandering furtively through the hills, suddenly I became part of the family.

The shepherd, whose name was Carlo, explained various things to me, telling me about other ancient places in the area that he had visited while grazing the goats. I mentally took note, thanked him, and I asked him if I could visit the interior of the church to admire the fresco, or what was left of it.

Carlo then told me that a group of students from an art institute in Rome recently visited the fresco, and he always willingly acted as a guide, as long as the goats are safely secured in the nearby enclosure. Why was this fresco so significant? Because it stood as one of the earliest examples of balloons in the history of art. It is indeed regrettable that our institutions were unable to undertake proper conservation measures for its preservation. Excitedly, I finally entered the church's space. The sun was in that part of the day where it hasn't yet decided whether to dive into the sunset or not. The perfect moment, because a ray of its soft and rosy light gently fell on the fresco: there it was, the "crusader knight".

The state of degradation of the only surviving fresco is already beyond any threshold of tolerance.

The Crusader Knight, a Gaetan Pastoral

You lost your head
on the road to Damascus
and to think
you were a portrait of a man
archetype of faith and deceit.

In the end, a Crusader
is a knight forever:
no longer the keeper of the Holy Grail
but a shepherd:
life conquers death.

Photo by Pasquale Di Sorbo in Don Paolo Capobianco, Federico II, Gaeta, 1995.
How the fresco appeared just twenty-five years ago (!) – Author's Note

11 | The Roman Cistern in the San Vitale Area

The San Vitale area of Gaeta, formally known as *Sant-Autale*, holds two additional traces of our past, one grimly industrial, the other archaeological. The first is the abandoned ENI oil refinery, with its smattering of abandoned fuel tanks; the second, not far from the refinery, is the Roman cistern of Gaeta.

The cistern is smaller than the one in Castellone di Formia, as well as two others of which I have heard only rumors – those, however, are reportedly located on private property and remain undeclared as historic sites, so take even their existence with a grain of salt.

Access to the cistern of San Vitale is via a small road that winds along the hillside, still displaying the original Roman pavement, although someone thoughtlessly poured cement over parts of it in recent times. Through a crack in a sidewall, you descend well-preserved steps to find yourself in a kind of "Batcave", supported by beautiful arches.

Bats dominate the area, and the small pools of water, some clear as the air itself, are astonishing themselves – water that ancient Romans will never again gather in their cups or utilize for irrigating their vineyards.

It would be truly wonderful to initiate a restoration of this archaeological site and return it to the community. Our city holds a wealth of archaeological treasures, some in plain sight (Serapo – Via della Madonnella[1]). Perhaps wealthy patrons interested in their restoration could be found?

[1] "It should have been named 'Via Madonnelle' instead, as when my grandmother still had gardens in the area that covered the entire Corso Italia up to the soccer stadium, there were remains of votive shrines (perhaps Roman or medieval), some of which were repainted with sacred images of mediocre workmanship that the popular piety used as reference points on the road." – Gennaro Tallini.

The current cattle track that allows access to the site: among the gravel, one can see the paving stones of the Roman road surface.

The external façade of the structure displays an architectural refinement that goes beyond a simple cistern: above the hydraulic work, there must have been an impressive building of considerable size.

*The cistern had an access for cleaning and maintenance, complete
with a ladder that allowed one to reach the bottom.*

Drops in the silence

Clung
to the cave of silence,
the word
centuries waiting
to flow once more.

*The masonry pillars and arches support a series of vaults: if it were a
church, we would say "6 barrel-vaulted naves with 5 bays each."*

Outside the structure, extensive sections of opus reticulatum *are still clearly visible. Near the large cistern, structures belonging to the city's electrical network have been installed. – Author's note*

12 | Villa Traniello

Adults my age will fondly recall many enjoyable soccer matches played at Villa Traniello,[1] the park nestled in the heart of the medieval district. Summer was the time for us locals to meet – and sometimes vigorously compete – with our fellow playmates who were vacationing in Gaeta. I'm not alluding to the contemporary weekend tourists; rather, I'm recalling those children who, accompanied by their families, used to relocate to Gaeta for the whole summer season. These were vacations from a bygone era, not as distant as one might think, but today, they seem light-years away.

When the legendary Super Santos PVC soccer ball ended up in the monument to the fallen's enclosure, there was always a commotion to decide who should go retrieve it. I must have jumped over the enclosure a million times, to say the least!

It has been more than a few years since I jumped over that enclosure. Life is strange: a gesture that was a habit until yesterday becomes something unusual before you know it, as the days pass...

In those days, the cannons still displayed their cylindrical, impressively-wide mouths, often regrettably filled with debris and other refuse. I daydreamed about the battles where they had thundered, launching fiery iron balls at enemy ships and troops. Who knows, with the appropriate precautions, they might still be functional and assist me in welcoming the morning with a resounding roar...

[1] The public garden was inaugurated in 1927 and dedicated to General Vincenzo Traniello in 1929.

The cannon that has fallen silent

You no longer speak to me, old cannon.
Perhaps you're offended,
for not having brought you
to my battles.

You would have scattered my mistakes,
my fears, my uncertainties,
in a single shot!

As we dreamt
of rebuilding the world
for fun:

the boy general
and his fire-breathing dragon.

I promise that when the war is over,
I will return to play:

nothing and no one
then, will be able to stop us.

One of the four Austro-Hungarian cannons (war spoils from WWI)
that complement the monument to the fallen, now diminished due to a
smaller Winged Victory, which, thanks to the generosity of some Gaetans,
replaced the monumental one that was plundered during the WWII.

| Coordinates

The below coordinates, once pasted on Google Maps, will lead you
the sites indicated in the book.

The Maritime Burial Ground
    41.226263704031055, 13.566118654796671
The Mithraeum
    41.25895281561517, 13.54370985850123
The Monastery of Colle Sant'Agata
    41.228409614043585, 13.56227603707098
The Monastery of Santo Spirito di Zannone in Gaeta
    41.23712888685312, 13.559724908235301
The Ducal Palace
    41.20888545217669, 13.584492491639802
The House of Sebastiano Conca
    41.22459081397077, 13.509309835219023
The Church of Sant'Angelo dei Marzi...
    41.25750201123288, 13.555181862204646
... and the Roman structure (Torcularium)
    41.2570745415365, 13.554688335750665
The Train of Memories
    41.223635341912406, 13.55950756393578
The Caves of Sant'Agostino
(Domus delle Acque Salse or Salt Water)
    41.238072056865306, 13.491135538922986
The Church of Saint Ambrose
    41.23949588334684, 13.565013375696104
The Roman Cistern in the San Vitale Area
    41.24132578123138, 13.549422852601197
Villa Traniello
    41.20999277368697, 13.583809451622935

| Conclusion

With this book, I hope to have piqued the curiosity of fellow towns-folk and tourists, to have accompanied the elderly or those who now reside far away back to the places they visited in their youth, and to have guided the young in discovering our territory.

The book is not intended to be a complete guide. For instance, the Rural Marian Chapels (Casalarga, Colle, Conca, Longato) are missing, as are countless other Roman and medieval ruins scattered throughout the Gaetan countryside, as well as in the medieval historic center and the "Borgo".

To narrate all the hidden treasures in Gaeta would require more than two books, let alone one. Other authors of great stature have come before me, and others will follow: Gaeta is a place where a sensitive soul can satisfy its longing for beauty. A moment rocked amidst the waves of the sea, the next with an ear attuned to the wind, which, among brambles and nameless ruins, speaks to you of a world that once was.

I invite readers to refer to the References provided at the end of this book, which will allow them to deepen their knowledge of the places celebrated in this text, and much more.

Above all, I invite each of you to "find in seeking," drawing forth the desire for discovery that, in the end, makes us men and women aware of our journey through the world's pathways.

| The Author

Born and raised in Italy as the son of a U.S. Navy officer stationed in Gaeta, Jason R. Forbus developed a profound affection and fascination for the history of his hometown from a young age. As he follows in the footsteps of the diverse peoples who have traversed this region, he champions the narrative of Gaeta—a city capable of captivating both ancient and contemporary travelers with its timeless charm.

Jason holds a degree in Sociology from the University of Aberdeen in Scotland. His career has encompassed roles with the U.S. Embassies in Italy and the United Kingdom, and he currently serves as a humanitarian worker for the United Nations.

Jason's literary voyage began in 2002, when he made a notable debut in the "Campiello Giovani" literary competition. There, he earned a place among the top 25 emerging authors nationwide and secured the top honor in the Lazio Region with his short story *Trovare il Cercare* (Finding in Seeking).

Since then, he has authored and published works in more than 12 languages, spanning essays, novels, children's books, and poetry. He also maintains a blog where he shares a diverse array of writings and reflections: http://cantasogni.blogspot.com.

| Main Collaborators

Gennaro Tallini, born in Gaeta in 1964, is a member of the CAI and SAT, holding a Doctorate in Philology. He has a diverse academic background, having worked as a researcher in Pisa and Lugano and served as a high school teacher. Currently, he teaches Italian literature at the University of Verona.

His primary focus lies in studying the literary production of authors from the Aurunca region, spanning the Middle Ages, the Renaissance, and the erudite 18th century. He has contributed significantly to this field, publishing papers and volumes on figures like Sebastiano Conca (*Civiltà Aurunca* 1997), Tomaso de Vio Cajetanus (*Rivista Storia di Letteratura Religiosa* 2010), Agostino Nifo (*Firenze* 2012; *Nuova Rivista Storica* 2014), Giovanni Tarcagnota (*Italianistica* 2011; *Roma* 2012; *Firenze* 2014; *Studi Veneziani* 2010; *Bibliologia* 2011; *Critica Letteraria* 2014; *Rivista di Tipofilologia* 2016; *Gaeta* 2016; *Roma* in c.d.s.). For Ali Ribelli Edizioni, he published works on Giovanni Tarcagnota, Antonio Minturno, Giovanni Camillo de' Spagnolis, and Luigi Capotorti.

Tallini's research extends to various periods, including the Renaissance and the 19th-century Risorgimento. He has authored works such as *Storia Geoletteraria dell'Area Aurunca nel Cinquecento* (Napoli 2008), *Musica e produzione artistica a Gaeta nel XVI secolo* (Studi Campani 2008), *Una lingua commune. Gaeta tra X e XVII secolo: storia e antiquaria, lingua e cultura* (Gaeta 2018), and critical editions of "Breve descrittione" by Pietro Rossetto (Raleigh [NC] 2016) and the war diary of a Bersagliere from Valtellina during the Siege of Gaeta in 1861 (Assedio di Gaeta e diacritica risorgimentale popolare, 2014).

Lino Sorabella, a registered journalist and tour guide for the Lazio Region, can be described as a storyteller of the region. He has conducted and continues to engage in scientific research on the territory, collaborating with universities and both public and private institutions. As a speaker at conferences and seminars and a contributing writer for various journalistic publications, he has authored several local-focused titles.

Additionally, he serves as a location manager for film productions in the Gulf of Gaeta region.

Paolo Di Tucci, a photographer for many years, has generously shared his professionalism and passion with the city of Gaeta, capturing its events, everyday moments, and breathtaking landscapes. In 2017, he was honored with the title of "Distinguished Italian Photographer" at the National Congress of the Italian Federation of Photographic Associations.

As a Media Partner for Gaeta's most significant events, including those of national importance, he organized two noteworthy exhibitions in 2019 and 2021, successfully showcasing the beauty of the "Pearl of the Tyrrhenian Sea."

Furthermore, Paolo is an advocate and instructor for both basic and advanced photography courses, collaborating with the most prominent organizations and associations in the region.

References

Special thanks to the "Salvatore Mignano" Municipal Library for enduring and supporting my explorations.

Agostino Di Mille ed Erasmo Valente, *Morte di Cicerone ad opera dei sicari di Marco Antonio nei pressi di Monte di Conca a Gaeta*, http://www.telefree.it/news.php?op=view&id=123122, 2018

Alessandro De Bonis, Chiara Canale, Cassandra Rita Russo, *Sviluppi storici nelle terre del basso Lazio: dalla preistoria all'avvento dei Longobardi*, Tre Bit Edizioni, Formia, 2019

Alfredo Saccoccio, *Fra' Diavolo. Vita ed imprese del colonnello Michele Pezza*, Gaeta, Ali Ribelli Edizioni, 2018

Alvise Schanzer, *Per la conoscenza dei dialetti del Lazio orientale: lo scadimento vocalico alla finale (primi risultati)*, in Contributi di filologia dell'Italia mediana, vol. 3, Foligno, Editoriale Umbra, 1989

Amedeo Maiuri, *Passeggiate Campane*, Rusconi Editore, 1990, Milano

Antonio Cesarale, *La Montagna Verde*, Edizioni del Comune di Gaeta, Gaeta, 2007

Antonio Ciano, *Jason Forbus nel Convento di Zannone a Gaeta*, https://www.youtube.com/watch?v=_vyRfPSvY6o, Gaeta, 2010

Antonio Ciano, *Per il Sangue di Tata*, Ali Ribelli Edizioni, Gaeta, 2018

Carlo Di Nitto, *I ruderi romani di San Vitale a Gaeta*, http://www.telefree.it/news.php?op=view&id=74403

Centro Storico Culturale (a cura di), *Sebastiano Conca (1680-1764)*, Centro Storico Culturale Gaeta, La Poligrafica, Gaeta, 1981

D. Onorato Gaetani d'Aragona, *Memorie Storiche della Città di Gaeta, II ediz.*, Stab.Tipo-Litografico della Minerva, Caserta, 1885

Eleonora Chinappi, *Tra Roma e Napoli: gli affreschi di S. Giovanni a mare e S. Angelo dei Marzi a Gaeta*, Arte Medievale IV serie – anno III, Università La Sapienza, Roma, 2013

Erasmo Vaudo (a cura di), Oltre l'immagine. Iconografia mariana a Gaeta dal XIII al XIX secolo, Gaeta, Gaetagrafiche, 1988

Fondazione Gaeta, Associazione "Mizar" (a cura di), *L'Abbazia di Santo Spirito di Zannone in Gaeta*, Ellegrafica, Gaeta, 2001

Francesco del Pozzone, *La festa della "MADONNA DI CONCA": Briciole di memoria storica*, http://www.telefree.it/news.php?op=view&id=99256, 2012

Francesco Di Chiappari, *Quel fischio mai dimenticato. Storia ad immagine della ferrovia Gaeta – Formia – Sparanise*, Consorzio Industriale Sud Pontino, Gaeta, 2017

Francesco Lofano, *La Decorazione Barocca dell'Abbazia di Montecassino in Mitteilungen Des Kunsthistorischen Institutes in Florenz in LX. Band – 2018, Heft 2*, Centro Di edizioni, Firenze, 2018

Gennaro "Rino" Tallini, *Gaeta una città nella Storia*, Edizioni del Comune di Gaeta, Gaeta, 2006

Giovanni Battista Federici, *Degli Antichi duchi e consoli o ipati della città di Gaeta*, Napoli, 1791

Giuseppe De Filippis, *Gaeta nella sinfonia di sole di acque di verde*, Graficart, Formia, 2004

Graziano Fronzuto, *Monumenti d'arte sacra a Gaeta: storia ed arte dei maggiori edifici religiosi di Gaeta*, Gaeta, Edizioni del Comune di Gaeta

Luigi Salemme, *Il Borgo di Gaeta: contributo alla storia locale*, I.T.E.R., Torino, 1939

Maria Stamegna, *Miti, leggende e folklore di Gaeta*, Ali Ribelli Edizioni, Gaeta, 2018

Maria Stamegna, *Silenziosi, ma sempre presenti*, Ali Ribelli Edizioni, Gaeta, 2019

Marisa de' Spagnolis, *Il Mitreo di Itri*, E.P.R.O, Brill, Leiden, 1980

Nicola Corcia, *Storia delle Due Sicilie dall'antichita più remota al 1789, Volume 1*, Tipografia Virgilio, Napoli, 1843

Nicola Magliocca, *Usi e costumi del popolo gaetano*, Centro Storico Culturale, Gaeta, 1994

Paolo Capobianco (Mons.), *FEDERICO II nell'ottavo centenario della nascita*, Edizioni Nuova Poligrafica, Gaeta, 1995

Paolo Manzi, *La Battaglia di Itri*, Ali Ribelli Edizioni, Gaeta, 2018

Pasquale Di Ciaccio, *Gaeta Guida Turistica*, Edizioni La Poligrafica, Gaeta, 1976

Pasquale Fantasia, *La rete stradale dell'antica Roma nell'Agro di Gaeta e gli avanzi delle vecchie costruzioni Romane nelle sue adiacenze*, Ed. Castellani, Roma, 1943

Piergiorgio Granata, *Gaeta: viaggio nell'arte: pittura, scultura e arti minori dal medioevo ad oggi*, Guida Editori, Napoli, 2004

Sabina Mitrano, *Gaeta e il suo nome rist*, Ali Ribelli Edizioni, Gaeta, 2019

Salvatore Antetomaso, *Salvatore Antetomaso, Storia e Studio del Dialetto Gaetano, Gaeta, 2013*

Salvatore Ferraro (Mons.), *Di una via aperta dal Censore L. Valerio Flacco nell'Agro Formiano*, Scuola tipografica salesiana, Roma, 1912

Wikipedia (a cura di), *Cappelle mariane rurali di Gaeta*, https://it.wikipedia.org/wiki/Cappelle_mariane_rurali_di_Gaeta